Americans Today and Yesterday

CONTENTS

NATIONAL GEOGRAPHIC
School Publishing
Hampton-Brown

Prefixes **dis-**, **pre-**, **in-**, **im-**

Look at each picture. Read the words.

Example:

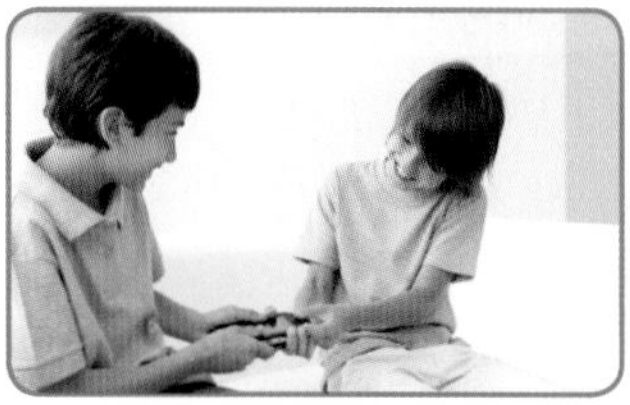

disagree

dislike

High Frequency Words

- America
- country
- father
- idea
- learn
- mother
- picture
- read
- seem
- word

Key Words

Look at the picture. Read the sentences.

A Good Idea

1. Sam's **father** and **mother** had an **idea** for a new life.
2. They moved to this **country**.
3. They **seem** to be happy now in **America**.
4. Their children **learn** to **read** in English and say new **words** each day.
5. Look at the **picture** they are painting.

What idea does the picture show?

Phonics Games
NGReach.com

We All Immigrated

by Imogene Cole
illustrated by Soud

Carlos and his family were leaving Mexico. They were moving to the United States. His family was packing, so boxes stood everywhere. The house was in disorder.

Cousin Berto came to help. Berto was a preteen, but he was nearly thirteen. Berto asked if people spoke Spanish where Carlos's family was going.

Carlos's father said that just a few people spoke Spanish. Carlos gasped in disbelief. How could his family immigrate to this place? He just spoke Spanish. How would he make friends?

His mother told him that he'd make friends. He'd learn to understand people.

At first Carlos felt glad to be in school in America. His teacher, Mrs. Ortez, spoke some Spanish. But he felt sad when he found that not one of his classmates spoke Spanish. Carlos sat by himself at lunchtime. He watched the other kids discussing things. He wished he could speak with them.

The weeks passed. Bit by bit, Carlos learned to read and say new words. He spoke with his classmates. Carlos often used a wrong word. Then he felt ashamed and wished he could disappear.

Mrs. Ortez spoke with Carlos. She said, “I hope you don’t dislike school. You seem sad, but you shouldn’t be. You understand what people say.”

Carlos said, “I want to speak like Nancy.” His sister was just in preschool, but she seemed to learn new words instantly.

Mrs. Ortez said, “You’ve been in this country a short time. Soon you’ll speak and read like you were born here.”

Carlos disagreed, but he didn’t say so. He didn’t want to seem disrespectful.

Mrs. Ortez wanted Carlos to feel happy. She had an idea for a project. She told the class, "I want each of you to ask your family when they immigrated to America. Tomorrow you can share what you learned."

The next day, Carlos spoke first. "My family came to America fifteen weeks ago."

Kento said, "My parents came from Japan, but I was born in America."

Paul spoke next. "My grandparents immigrated here fifty years ago. They came from Poland."

Shawn's family took an indirect path to America. "My parents' families came from Africa to South America a long time ago," he explained. "Then my grandparents left and came here way before I was born."

Amy said, "My parents were born in the United States, but both their families came from Scotland in the 1700s."

Grace said, "All of us are like Carlos. Our families immigrated, too!"

Carlos smiled. He said, "We all are alike. Our families all immigrated."

Then Carlos asked, “Mrs. Ortez, can we paint a big picture? We can show where our families came from.”

Paul said, “That’s a good idea!”

Mrs. Ortez said, “Yes! I invite you all to paint!”

Prefixes dis-, pre-, in-, im-

Read these words.

disorderly	preheat	imperfect	disorganized	pretend
inside	disagree	preview	messy	inform

Find the words with the prefixes **dis-**, **pre-**, **in-**, and **im-**. Use letters to build them.

d i s o r d e r l y

Talk Together

The room is disorderly.

Choose words from the box above to describe the room in the picture.

Suffixes -**er**, -**or**, -**less**, -**ness**

Look at each picture. Read the word.

Example:

zipp**er**

read**er**

bak**er**

act**or**

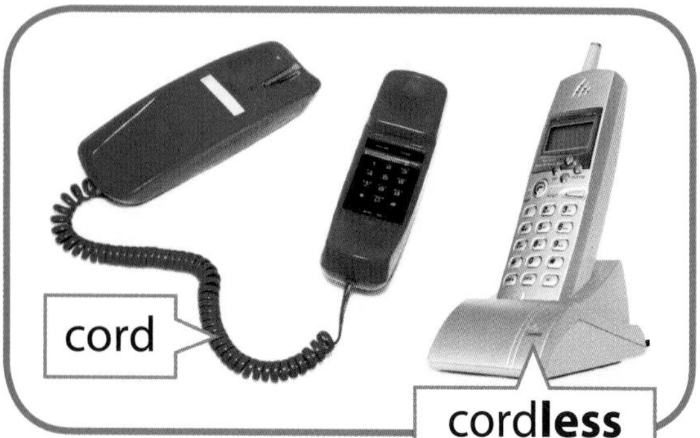

dark**ness**

Key Words

Look at the pictures. Read the sentences.

High Frequency **Words**

- America
- country
- father
- idea
- learn
- mother
- picture
- read
- seem
- word

Southwest Desert Pictures

1. This **mother**, **father**, and children are in a desert in **America**.
2. They are in the Southwest of this **country**.
3. They **read** a map to **learn** where to go, which is a good **idea**.
4. A desert may **seem** like a painted **picture**.
5. The **word** *dry* tells what a desert is like.

What do you think the people are saying?

GO! **Phonics Games**

NGReach.com

The Timeless Southwest

by Sky Barker

The United States of America is a large country. The Southwest is one part of it. People have different ideas about which states are part of the Southwest. The map shows one idea. The Southwest appears in yellow on the map. Which states make up the Southwest? Have you been a visitor to any of these states?

Visiting the Southwest

The Southwest has countless visitors each year. Much of the Southwest is dry, sunny, and rainless for long stretches of time. In spring, it often rains and flowers bloom. Then the dryness returns, and the land is baked by the hot summer sun.

Many people like to visit deserts in the Southwest. Hikers, campers, and bike riders spend time here, looking at the amazing sights and taking pictures.

Doesn't this photograph seem like a priceless painted picture? It shows part of the Painted Desert. The Painted Desert is one of the deserts in the Southwest. Why do you think the word *painted* is part of this desert's name?

People of the Southwest

Native Americans lived here first. Spanish explorers came in the 1500s. Later, people from Spain and Mexico moved here in large numbers. People came from other parts of the world, too.

Native Americans are an important part of the Southwest today. Some make a living showing their skills to visitors. Rather than reading about Native American dancers, the spectators in this photo are watching a live dancer. This Native American man is doing a hoop dance.

Native Americans keep the old skills alive. How? Artists act as teachers. A weaver teaches some young people the art of weaving. A potter teaches children the art of making pottery. Look at the photos. What might this modern-day weaver be weaving? What is the potter making?

Many different people make their homes in the Southwest. Some live and work in cities and suburbs. Some work the land—farmers growing crops, ranchers raising sheep and cattle. Some are drawn to the richness *under* the land. Mining, oil, and gas are important industries in the Southwest.

Food of the Southwest

The first people of the Southwest, the Native Americans, grew beans, corn, and squash. These foods are still popular. The greenness of the squash in this photo makes it look as good as it tastes!

Settlers from Mexico added peppers to the cooking. Adding peppers adds spiciness to food. Barbecue and stews are other foods you'll find in the Southwest. What foods from the Southwest have you eaten?

The sun will soon set, leaving this southwestern desert in darkness. But it will rise again tomorrow on the enchanting land of the Southwest.

Suffixes -er, -or, -less, -ness

Read these words.

baker	explore	visitor	rainless	hiker
dryness	cloudless	corn	brightness	sandiness

Find the words with the suffixes **-er**, **-or**, **-less**, and **-ness**. Use letters to build them.

b a k e r

Talk Together

Choose words from the box above to tell your partner what the hikers like about the Southwest desert.

The hikers like the brightness of the cloudless desert.

A Desert in America

Look at the picture with a partner. Take turns reading the clues and pointing to answers.

1. Find one hiker in the dryness of the desert who is talking on a cordless phone.
2. Find the painter painting the sky inexactly.
3. Find the word *elevator* in the picture.
4. Find a father disagreeing with his preteen. (Hint: This preteen wants to learn how to ride.)
5. Find a visitor who dislikes imperfect fruit.
6. Find a mother with two dogs that seem harmless.

Acknowledgments
Grateful acknowledgment is given to the authors, artists, photographers, museums, publishers, and agents for permission to reprint copyrighted material. Every effort has been made to secure the appropriate permission. If any omissions have been made or if corrections are required, please contact the Publisher.

Photographic Credits
CVR (bg) Mingei International Museum/Art Resource, Inc. (bl) DreamPictures/VC/Blend Images/Getty Images. **2** (bl) Bill Noll/iStockphoto. (br) Margot Petrowski/Shutterstock. (cl) Taratorki/Shutterstock. (tl) Sigrid Olsson/PhotoAlto/Corbis. (tr) Jose Luis Pelaez Inc/Getty Images. **3** Liz Garza Williams/Hampton-Brown/National Geographic School Publishing. **15** (bl) Mark Rose/iStockphoto. (cr) Liz Garza Williams/Hampton-Brown/National Geographic School Publishing. **16** (bl) Brett Stoltz/Shutterstock. (cl) Kelly Cline/iStockphoto. (cr) Cindy Charles/PhotoEdit. (tl) mete1958/Shutterstock. (tr) PhotoDisc/Getty Images. (bc) Pakhnyushcha/Shutterstock. (br) James P. Blair/National Geographic Image Collection. **17** (b) Liz Garza Williams/Hampton-Brown/National Geographic School Publishing. (tl) Table Mesa Prod/Index Stock RF/age fotostock. (tr) S.M./Shutterstock. **18-19** Paul B. Moore/Shutterstock. **20** (c) Kate Thompson/National Geographic Image Collection. (cr) Cathrine Wessel/Corbis. (tl) Marc Schlossman/Getty Images. **21** Naegele,FRPS/age fotostock. **22** Peter V. Bianchi/National Geographic Image Collection. **23** Craig Lovell/Corbis. **24** (cr) Buddy Mays/Alamy Images. (tl) Marilyn Angel Wynn/Corbis. **25** (t) Dean Conger/National Geographic Image Collection. (tl) Nancy Carter/North Wind Picture Archives. (tl) Andrew Dean/iStockphoto. (tr) Joel Sartore/National Geographic Image Collection. **26** (cl) Artville. (cr) Piotr Tomicki/Shutterstock. **27** (c) Joe Gough/Shutterstock. (tl) mihalec/Shutterstock. (tr) PhotoDisc/Getty Images. **28** Anton Foltin/Shutterstock. **29** (bl) Tom Bean/Getty Images. (br) Liz Garza Williams/Hampton-Brown/National Geographic School Publishing.

Illustrator Credits
4-14 Soud; **30-31** Peter Grosshauer

National Geographic School Publishing
Hampton-Brown
www.NGSP.com

Printed in the USA.
Quad Graphics, Leominster, MA

ISBN:978-0-7362-8084-6

17 18 19
10 9 8 7 6